Here's Looking at You

Contents

Page

Malorie Blackman Biography

Malorie's tips for writing a great story.

1. *Start with a simple idea for the plot.*

2. *Make each character believable by knowing their appearance, likes, dislikes and so on.*

3. *Make sure the story is exactly the sort of thing you can imagine happening to these characters.*

4. *Plan what will happen in each chapter.*

5. *Know where the plot is going by working out the beginning, middle and end.*

8 Feb 1962 Born in Beckenham, London

1967 Starts Churchfields Primary School, Beckenham

1973 Starts Honor Oak Grammar School, Peckham

1980 Starts work in computer industry. Studies computing at evening classes.

1988 Starts writing in evenings after work – science fiction stories for adults

1990 First book published – *Not So Stupid* (book of short stories for teenagers)

1991 Takes year off work to try writing full time

1992 *Hacker* published – decides to b ecome full-time writer

1994 *Hacker* wins Young Telegraph Children's Book of the Year award

1995 Daughter Elizabeth born

2000 *Pig-heart Boy* wins award for Best Children's Drama

2001 *Noughts and Crosses* published – first novel for young adults

2002 *The Amazing Birthday*, a play, was performed at the Polka Theatre

2004 *Cloud Busting* published – a story in verse

Most importantly, READ. In my opinion, if you don't read, you can't write.

When I started writing, a couple of people in my family told me I was wasting my time... They said I would never get published. They said "There aren't any black writers'!

Find your own style and your own way of expressing yourself. Don't copy anyone else.

"*Noughts and Crosses* must be the most original book I have ever read. It's intelligent, emotional and imaginatively wicked. *Benjamin Zephaniah*"

"Blackman is becoming a bit of a national treasure. *The Times*"

A Wretchedly Brief Biography concerning the Shadowy Life of Mr Lemony Snicket

If you are expecting to read the life story of the mysterious author Mr Lemony Snicket, then you may be disappointed. Of course, this biography should reveal his whole history, but it will not because it cannot. An exhaustive amount of research – a phrase here meaning "lots of nosing around" – has revealed only a dismal drizzle of information about him. It has also dug up a most unfortunate truth. So, please feel free to leg it to the library and read something jolly.

The elusive Lemony Snicket

It is said that, as a child, Lemony Snicket studied taxidermy – a word meaning "the distasteful art of stuffing dead bodies". It isn't surprising that he pens such dismal tales without a single happy ending. He admits that he "cannot understand why booksellers want such melancholy books on their shelves." Mr Snicket steeps himself in secrecy. He will only be photographed from behind. He never turns up at interviews and sends a chap in a gaudy shirt instead. Lemony Snicket is a riddle, or he would be had he ever existed.

Why do you think Lemony Snicket likes to remain mysterious?

Now I must reveal the unfortunate truth. The chap in the gaudy shirts is another author. His name is Daniel Handler. It is possible – no, it is probable – that Mr Handler *is* Lemony Snicket.

Daniel Handler was born in San Francisco in the USA in 1970. As a child he read Roald Dahl and played the accordion "... to drive his parents crazy". He went to college in New York and began to write his first novel for adults. It took six years to get it published.

He is happy to be interviewed about his love of writing, opera, scary things and playing in a rock band. Yet, when asked, "Is Lemony Snicket your pen name?" he replies evasively, "No, my pen's name is Alphonse."

In 1999 Daniel Handler began to write mock horror stories for children. *A Series of Unfortunate Events* is frighteningly funny – a cat's cradle of good and evil. When he created the ill-fated Baudelaire orphans, he also created their shadowy author. This made the books doubly mysterious, doubly thrilling. What a stroke of citric – a word here meaning "sharp" – genius. They became a huge success and have been made into a film; something he finds "mind-boggling".

So, this wretchedly brief biography has spilled the beans. But what matter if Daniel Handler is Lemony Snicket, or vice versa come to that? Mr Snicket has warned that there will be thirteen books charting the evil events surrounding the Baudelaire orphans. For some, they are alarming. For others, they are the bees' knees – a phrase here meaning "just brilliant"!

Maureen Haselhurst

What kind of person do you think Daniel Handler is?

A Writer's Horror Story (or How Not to Do It)

I arrive at the station.
There's no one to meet me.
Phone the name I've been given.
That person's on holiday.
I'm put on hold, for what seems like forever.

When at last someone speaks, they give me directions.
"Turn left, left, right, left, then right, right, then south!
It's a good hour's walk but the view is amazing."
So I pick up my bag, full of books, sheets and objects.
It weighs half a ton and I'm already tired.

Stumble and fumble my way to the library.
I'm late and I'm knackered.
Why didn't they meet me?
"The kids are all here. Go straight in and meet them."
"Can I go to the toilet?"

"But the kids are all restless. And there're no adults
with them – they've gone for a coffee."
"How many children?"
"Two hundred and eighty."
"But a workshop's for thirty. I explained when you phoned me."

"Well, they're here now. You'll wow them. You've no need to
worry."
"I'll just do a session. How old are the children?"
"From three months to sixteen."
"But my talks are for the nine plus – as I said in my letter."
"But now you'll reach everyone. That's so much the better!"

Why did she write this poem? Where was she speaking?

"Have the children read any of my books?"
"I don't think they have – no."
"So they don't even know me?"
"I'm sure they'll still love it."
"Will my books be on sale at all, after the session?"

"Our children won't buy them, if they're not Harry Potter.
So we didn't get any – I'm sure you don't mind."
But I do, yes I do. I DO mind, you will find.
"I sent in my invoice, I hope that you got it."
"Ah… Er… there's a problem. I'm afraid we forgot it.

Wait for eight months and we'll happily pay.
Let's not talk about money. Let's just have a good day!"
"If you don't mind me asking, why was I invited?"
"We had surplus budget. And it was use it or lose it.
And Jacqueline Wilson was busy."

"Can I at least have some water?"
"You didn't bring your own?"
A sigh and a wish that I'd stayed in my home.
"We love your Ms Wiz books. We think you're all right!
But I must say Mr Blacker, we thought you were white!!"

(This is a true story!)

by Malorie Blackman (Mrs)!!

What have you learned about inviting an author to speak?

Some of Malorie Blackman's Books

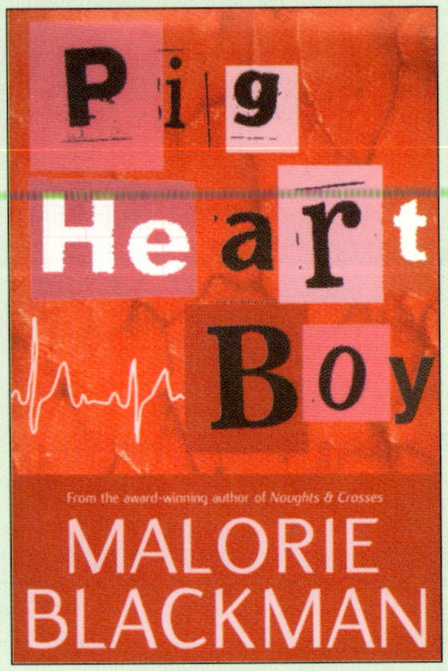

Peacemaker

"Michela Corbin, what did I just say?"

The class began to snigger. I looked up dismayed. There, right in front of my desk, stood Teacher Faber. I stared up at her, blinking with confusion. I hadn't even seen her coming! I tried to cover my literature screen with my hand but the teacher was too quick for me. She snatched up my screen and started to read the story I'd been writing. I groaned. I was in deep, *deep* trouble. Again!

"Michela Corbin, you are supposed to be writing an essay on section four-one-five of the Peace Treaty between the Alliance and the Inthral Sector. Not this… this… *this*!" Teacher Faber waved my lit. screen under my nose with disdain.

"I'm sorry. I'll erase it." I grabbed for my screen. Teacher Faber snatched it back.

"Let us take a look at what has so captured your attention," said the teacher, her tone really sarcastic. "Are you ready for this, class?" she asked. "*I spun around, quick as a Pogett snake. Davin lunged at me with her laz-sword. Immediately I swung my weapon down to parry her thrust. The sound of laser beam on laser beam zinged almost musically. With a furious roar, Davin whipped her laz-sword upwards towards my head. I ducked and stepped back simultaneously. I didn't want to hurt her but one touch from the laz-sword was lethal – and I wasn't about to die. I…*" Teacher Faber stopped reading, but not before my face was on fire. Half the class were in fits of laughter. The other half were glaring at me, disapprovingly.

"This tish-tosh is not just nonsense, it's dangerous nonsense. I told you the last time that you'd had your final warning. Now you'll go on report. Again," said Teacher Faber with satisfaction.

"Oh please, you can't. My mother will go nuts! I'll do the essay. I'll stay behind and work late. I'll…"

"Not another word," interrupted the teacher. "You're on report and that's final. And I shall make sure that your mother sees this … this story of yours."

Why do you think Michela's teacher is so angry with her?

My blood ran icy cold. "You can't do that..." I whispered.

"Watch me," said Teacher Faber. "I don't know what's wrong with you, Michela. You persist with writing these kinds of stories..."

"They're adventure stories," I protested. "They're just fiction..."

"You humans are supposed to abhor violence of any kind – even in stories," said Teacher Faber. "And yet Michela, you insist on reading forbidden books like *Treasure Island* and *The Three Musketeers* and on writing this kind of fantastical, dangerous foolishness."

It wasn't my fault I read forbidden books. If they weren't forbidden in the first place, then I wouldn't get into trouble for reading them! Mother owned an impressive collection of nineteenth- and twentieth-century fiction books, most of them now classified as forbidden. She kept them locked up in dura-glass cases and it'd taken me ages to get at them without Mother knowing. She called them "a good investment" – whatever that meant. I called them a good read. I didn't see the point in owning books if you didn't read them. The trouble was, Mother didn't see it like that. I'd been caught with Mother's books more than once and the last time, Mother threatened to burn them all if I was caught with just one of them again. So instead of

 What has Michela done wrong?

reading them, I'd taken to writing my own – but that seemed to get me into even worse trouble!

"I won't read or write any more," I pleaded. "Please don't report me."

Teacher Faber keyed in some commands on the console that was situated on her stomach. Her fingers moved so quickly, they were a blur.

"It is done," Teacher Faber moved away. "A full report has been transmitted to Commander Newton and to your mother."

I scowled at her. Rotten, Pogett-brained, Valunian weasel! I groaned. What was my mother going to say?

* * *

"Teacher Faber sent me yet another demerit report on you today."

"Mother, I can explain... "

Mother flopped down into her favourite recliner and kicked off her shoes. "Michela, I don't want to hear it," she sighed. "I've reasoned with you, pleaded with you, argued until I'm blue."

"It was only a story, Mother," I said quietly.

"A story! Why can't you write stories about proper subjects? What's wrong with peace and diplomacy and friendship? Why must you revel in violence?"

"I don't," I said furiously. "They're only stories, Mother... "

"They're a way of thinking. They're a way of *being*," my mother replied. "You persist in embarrassing me in front of my colleagues. Think of what your father would say if he was still alive."

And with that one single argument, Mother forced me to shut up and not argue.

An uncomfortable silence filled the room.

"Michela, have you been recoding your Peacemaker?"

"Of course not!" I blustered.

After the *Treasure Island* incident, I'd been sent to Doctor Bevan to have my Peacemaker checked out. Everyone had a Peacemaker permanently attached to the inside of their left wrist on their eleventh birthday. There were no exceptions made. The Peacemaker was a small, grey disk which looked like one of those old-fashioned buttons people used to fasten their

What does her mother do? What is the Peacemaker?

clothes. Doctor Bevan explained that it was a behavioural inhibitor – supposed to ensure that the non-aggression we'd all been taught for the last century was more than just a lesson. The Peacemaker was supposed to make sure that it was physically impossible for us humans to be aggressive. No more wars, no more fights, we couldn't hurt each other any more. Only it didn't stop there. Books and films that had once been considered classics had now been banned. And more and more things these days were taken as signs of belligerence, like talking, laughing and singing too loudly – as I do all three, I'm constantly on report! Take last feast day, for example. We had Caen-Hal flowers from Rigel-4 for dessert. Caen-Hal flowers are most people's favourite food, a treat we only have once a year because they're so difficult and expensive to grow. Jeanette Peters tried to pinch mine and because I protested I was put on report and hauled up in front of Mother.

"How come it's all right for Jeanette to steal my food but it's not all right for me to stop her?" I asked angrily.

"Jeanette was wrong too," said Mother. "But you were more wrong! Your reaction could have led to violence. And as my daughter, Michela, you should know better."

 Why does everybody have to wear a Peacemaker?

And that was the problem really. I was always letting Mother down – and we both knew it.

Mother shook her head sadly. "Why do you do it? I read your story, Michela. Is that really what's in your head – in spite of everything I've tried to teach you?"

"It was just a story, Mother," I whispered unhappily.

"And the part where you were fighting with the laz-sword?" Mother asked.

"I put that in because it's the only weapon I've seen a hologram of," I said.

"You told me that you wanted to train in Je-kan-ia for the exercise, to teach you balance and co-ordination. It's obvious what's in your mind as you use the Kan-ia – you pretend it's a real weapon instead of the plastic stick it is. I forbid you to practise that so-called sport in the future," said Mother.

"But it's the only thing I'm any good at," I protested. Don't take that away from me. Not that as well, I thought desperately.

"That's enough. You're not to practise Je-kan-ia any more and that's final."

From the look on Mother's face, I knew she really meant it.

"And you can go to Doctor Bevan right this minute and get your Peacemaker checked out. And if you have been tampering with it … "

"CON ONE! CON ONE! Captain Corbin to the bridge immediately. Captain Corbin to the bridge."

Mother was interrupted in mid-sentence. She slipped her shoes back on to her feet and within seconds she was out the door. I stared after her. What was going on? What had happened to take us from Condition Four – our usual state – to Condition One, which was only used for extreme, imminent danger? Usually the Cons moved up sequentially – not a jump from Four to One.

I was used to Mother, as captain of the ship, being called away at a moment's notice. At first it'd seemed exciting to have such an important mother – captain of the *Kitabu*, one of the most prestigious ships in the Alliance fleet. Recently the excitement had faded away to leave something else, something less noble, in its place. I hardly ever saw her. And it seemed to me that Mother was always Captain Corbin first and being my mother came a long way down the list. I didn't want to feel the way I did and I tried to stop myself but I couldn't help it.

Why did Michela tamper with her Peacemaker?

"Come on, Michela," I muttered, trying to pull myself together. What should I do now? I glanced down at my Peacemaker. Whatever the emergency was, it'd saved me from getting into real trouble.

"What's going on?" I wondered out loud.

There was only one way to find out. I left the room and headed up to the bridge. Maybe I could sneak in without Mother seeing me.

But the moment I stepped on to the bridge, I gasped, then froze. There, directly in front of the *Kitabu* was the biggest ship I'd ever seen. Only a small portion of it filled the entire viewscreen. It must have had some kind of sensor-jamming device to appear before us like this without any warning.

There was no way anyone would throw me off the bridge. All eyes were on the colossal ship before us.

"Ensign Natsua, activate the universal decoder. Open a channel," Mother said. She was standing before the viewer on the bridge, her face solemn.

"This is Captain Corbin of the Alliance ship, *Kitabu*. We come in peace. Our mission is to negotiate trade and route lines through this sector. Do you understand?"

Each encounter with a new alien species called for Mother or Commander Newton, her second-in-command, to issue a similar blurb. The idea was that the alien ship would analyse the words spoken, so that any further communication to them could be translated. That's the way our universal decoder worked as well.

Everyone on the bridge looked tense. This was always the worst moment of dealing with alien species.

After only a few moments, the alien ship disappeared off one half of my viewer to be replaced by the face and upper body of one of the alien crew. And such a face I'd never seen before. My breath caught in my throat and refused to budge. The alien's face held only one eye in what was presumably its forehead. Its nose dominated its face, moving in a series of ridges downwards and outwards. It had lips – different from humans but similar enough to be recognisable as such. But the thing that made me stare without blinking, the thing that turned my stomach over was the

 What is different about Michela?

alien's skin. It was transparent. I could see grey liquid running through tiny canals in its body. I could see the tops of two organs, one either side of its upper body contracting and expanding. The two organs had to be the alien's hearts. The whole thing looked strange, bizarre – and totally disgusting!

"This is Captain Corbin of the Alliance ship, *Kitabu*. We come in peace. Do you understand?" Mother repeated. She didn't bat an eyelid at the look of the thing before her.

"I am Fflqa-Tur, a Chamrah knight. And I understand perfectly," the alien replied. "You have entered our sector without permission and must pay the price."

"The price?" Mother questioned sharply.

"Our ships are now at war," said Fflqa-Tur.

Malorie Blackman

The Computer's First Christmas Card

Jollymerry
hollyberry
jollyberry
merryholly
happyjolly
jollyjelly
jellybelly
bellymerry
hollyheppy
jollyMolly
marryJerry
merryHarry
happyBarry
heppyJarry
boppyheppy
berryjorry
jorryjolly

 How does the layout help you read and understand it?

moppyjelly
Mollymerry
Jerryjolly
bellyboppy
jorryhoppy
hollymoppy
Barrymerry
Jarryhappy
happyboppy
boppyjolly
jollymerry
merrymerry
merrymerry
merryChris
ammerryasa
Chrismerry
asMERRYCHR
YSANTHEMUM

Edwin Morgan

Why are there nonsense words?

Lost on Level Seven

I'm playing on my Megadrive,
Don't ask me what it cost.
I'm up to Level Seven now,
But don't you know I'm lost?

Disfigured ghouls and demons
Are chasing after me,
And a manic wrestler broke my back,
Back on Level Three.

There's grizzly little gremlins
Down on Level One
That want to rip my heart out
Just for a bit of fun.

There's a line of laughing lizards
Down on Level Two
Who seem to think my eyeballs
Should be bubbling in their stew.

I told you about the wrestler
I met on Level Three
It's true he snapped my vertebrae –
Now I'll never learn to ski.

Level Four looked easy –
Just a never-ending maze;
Till it filled with gibbering goblins,
Slobbering and crazed.

 Would you like to play? Which Level would you most like to avoid?

When I crawled in to Level Five,
I was just glad to be alive.
It's like a nightmare birthday party
With all your enemies invited –
Here in the Megadrive.

I'm losing all my energy –
I need my Weetabix
To beat the cloud of toxic gas
That lurks on Level Six.

So here I am still sitting here,
Lost on Level Seven:
I started out at one o'clock
And now it's gone eleven.

I don't hear you say it's teatime;
I don't know my mates have knocked.
I'm stuck inside this Megadrive
With all the exits blocked.

Now you know the reason
That I just can't hear you –
I've turned into a zombie,
And now I'm turning blue!

Dave Ward

What else was happening while the writer was stuck in the game?

Streetwise

Contents **Page**

Philip Ridley

Philip Ridley was born on 29 December 1964 in the East End of London and still lives in the same block of flats as he was born in. He studied fine art at St Martin's College and has exhibited his work across Europe. He says that he has always drawn and written stories and that he used to tell his younger brother bedtime stories to help him go to sleep.

Philip writes for both adults and children and he has written play and film scripts as well as novels. He says his favourite book is *Stig of the Dump* by Clive King. Of Ridley's children's novels, *Krindlekrax* (1991) won the Smarties Prize, *Kasper in the Glitter* (1994) was nominated for the Whitbread Prize and *Scribbleboy* (1997) was shortlisted for the Carnegie Medal. Philip Ridley wrote his first novel (unpublished) when he was seven and his first published novel when he was 19.

He sets his stories in places that he knows and bases his characters on people who he knows. He tries to write about things that are interesting for children today. His books deal with themes like bullying, homelessness and family break-ups, all from a child's point of view. As well as being a writer and painter, he has worked in a pie and mash shop, a betting office and a chip shop and as a DJ in a night club.

His three top tips for becoming a professional writer are:

1. Read as much as you can.
2. Write as much as you can.
3. Keep a diary.

What do you think is the most interesting fact about Philip Ridley? Why?

Do Philip Ridley and Malorie Blackman have anything in common?

Who's Who in Krindlekrax

Ruskin Splinter lives with his parents, Wendy and Winston, in a terraced house in Lizard Street. It is the end of the school year and Mr Lace, Ruskin's class teacher, is casting the end-of-year play. Ruskin desperately wants to be the hero but his appearance is against him. He is thin with knobbly knees, a mass of frizzy red hair and wears thick glasses. At the auditions, Mr Lace gives Elvis Cave the hero's part. Of course, Ruskin is a far better actor but Elvis looks the part. Elvis and Sparky Walnut are two of Ruskin's classmates. They all started at St George's School on the same day. That's when they met Corky Pigeon, the school caretaker. At first, all three boys were great friends. Since then, Elvis has grown into the local tough boy and Sparky follows him like a shadow. So now, Ruskin's only real friend is Corky. Corky has taken Ruskin home for a cup of tea and, to cheer him up, has promised to tell Ruskin why the bricks in Lizard Street are so dark and the pavement so full of cracks.

Now read on ...

What do we learn about Elvis from the summary?

Something in the Sewers

"It's quite a story," Corky said. "More strange than Elvis growing into the window-smasher of Lizard Street. It's a story so strange, you might not believe it."

"I'll believe it," Ruskin said. "Tell me."

"Well," Corky said, "you know when you sometimes feel a rumbling in the ground under Lizard Street? And people tell you it's a tube train going by beneath?"

"Yes," Ruskin said.

"Well, it's not a tube train," Corky said. "It's the thing that lives in the sewers. It's the thing that comes up through the largest drain in the street. It comes at night, when we're asleep, and cracks pavements with its gigantic tail, scorching bricks with its fiery breath and digging holes in roads with its sharp claws."

"What is it?" Ruskin asked breathlessly.

"Krindlekrax," Corky replied...

What sort of a creature do you think Krindlekrax is?

Corky dunked a chocolate biscuit in his tea and licked it thoughtfully. He licked it until all the chocolate had gone, then threw the biscuit away and took another from the packet.

"What's Krindlekrax?" Ruskin asked.

"To tell the story properly," Corky said, "I'll have to go back ten years."

"Ten years!" Ruskin said. "That's before I was born."

"That's right," Corky said, wiping chocolate from his lips. "Ten years ago a lot of things were different."

"What things?"

"Well," Corky said, "the pavements weren't cracked for one thing. And the brickwork wasn't dark and the road didn't have holes and bumps in."

"Because ... because Krindlekrax wasn't around then?" suggested Ruskin.

"That's right," Corky said, taking another biscuit from the packet. "And I wasn't caretaker of St George's School."

"You weren't!" Ruskin said, amazed.

"Oh, I know what you think," Corky said, dunking the biscuit in his tea and starting to lick the chocolate. "You think I've always been a caretaker and I've always worn a white overall and had grey hair and walked with a walking stick. But that's not true. Ten years ago, my hair was black and I walked without a limp, and I didn't work at St George's School."

"So where did you work?" Ruskin asked, sipping his tea.

"In the sewers," Corky replied.

"The sewers!" Ruskin exclaimed, nearly dropping his cup.

"Yes, my dear boy. The sewers. Underground where all the dirty water is. In the smelly dark. At least, that's how most people think of it. But I never thought of it like that. For me it was beautiful. The walls are bright green and the water makes a gentle, trickling noise. There are chambers big as cathedrals, and waterfalls so high you can't see the top. And when you speak, your voice echoes round you a million times until your ears ring and you get giddy. It's another world down there and I loved everything about it. I felt like an explorer. Being down there was a true adventure for me, my dear boy."

How are Corky's views about the sewers different from most people's?

"If it was dark," Ruskin said, "how did you see?"

"I'll show you," Corky replied.

Corky got up and went over to a wardrobe. He opened the door, removing something wrapped in newspaper, then returned to the table.

"What's that?" Ruskin asked.

"Open it and see," Corky said, handing it to him.

The newspaper was very old and had turned yellow. It smelt of damp and dust.

Carefully, Ruskin peeled away the paper, like peeling an onion, and inside he found a tin helmet with a torch stuck on the front.

"I wonder if it still works," Corky said. And he reached over and flicked a switch on top of the torch.

The torch lit up.

Corky took the helmet from Ruskin and put it on.

Why is the play script on pages 8–9 shorter than the narrative?

Corky's Secret

SCENE 8: CORKY'S LIVING ROOM

The room is suggested by armchair, cooker, sideboard and some framed photos. Corky pours hot water from kettle into teapot, then brings pot to chair. He sits and smiles at Ruskin, who is cross-legged on the floor.

Ruskin So … tell me!

Corky Tell you what, my boy?

Ruskin You know! What caused the holes? And cracks. And burnt bits of wall.

Corky Told you. Its claws. Its tail. Its breath.

Ruskin But what is … *it?*

Corky Oh… that's my secret.

Ruskin You can tell me. I'm your friend, ain't I?

Corky My very best.

Ruskin And you're my very best, too. Ain't you, Corky?

Corky For ever and always.

Ruskin And for ever and always friends shouldn't have secrets.

What does the story tell you about Corky that the play script doesn't?

Slight pause.

Well, should they?

Corky Look in that top drawer, my boy. Go on!

Ruskin goes to drawer and removes a steel helmet with torch on.

Ruskin What is it?

Corky I used to wear it.

Ruskin For what?

Corky The job I had. Before I was a caretaker.

Ruskin Before you were a caretaker?

Corky Well, I wasn't born a caretaker, you know. And I wasn't born with white hair and a face full of wrinkles either. I know it may come as a bit of a shock, my boy, but once … I was young.

Ruskin Can't imagine you young.

Corky Can't imagine it myself any more. But young I was. A young sewer inspector.

Ruskin Sewer inspector!

Corky My job. I'd put that thing on and – Here!

Puts helmet on.

How does Ruskin persuade Corky to tell him his secret?

Ruskin the Hero

1. Into the monster's lair.

3. The rats have got it!

2. Corky's stick!

4. But not for long!

5. Oh no, it's Krindlekrax!

7. Ruskin makes a stand.

6. He's coming out!

8. Our hero wins the day.

Rats

Mum said the hall was draughty,
the ceilings too low,
back bedroom too small.
And Dad said the walls
weren't straight; and the lane was dirty:
I never noticed; it was just home.

And the lane-end had a brook
and a big hill
with black gravelly stuff that slithered you all
down one side.
Adults said it looked
like an old slag-heap – spoil showed still
where the grass hadn't grown.
They called it the Tip, but it was
   Kanchenjunga,
dangerous and rocky in Winter, a wide
waste with yetis; or, in Summer,
hot rocks with Indians who died
in thousands each day.

And the brook, they say,
is smelly, no fit place
for you to play in. Look! They say,
A rat's under the bridge there!
And, sure enough, a whiskered face
points out at me and, scared
by something, slips sleekly long-bodied
down through the furtive stream,
the water unmuddied
as the long tail trails
ripples behind it.

What did you think about the poem when you heard it?

And you mustn't mind it if I dream
of those forbidden rats, and build
dams out of mud, to bail
the water into new-dug channels;
for my canals
carry great ships all round the world,
and mutineers are killed,
strange ports are sighted, slaves disembark
with sea-chests full of gold.

And have I told you?
Graham Cashmore's got a new flat
the other side of the park;
it's got its own lift
and boxes downstairs for the post
and a balcony, with stranglers and ghosts
making the curtains shift ...
But he hasn't got any rats.

Tony Charles

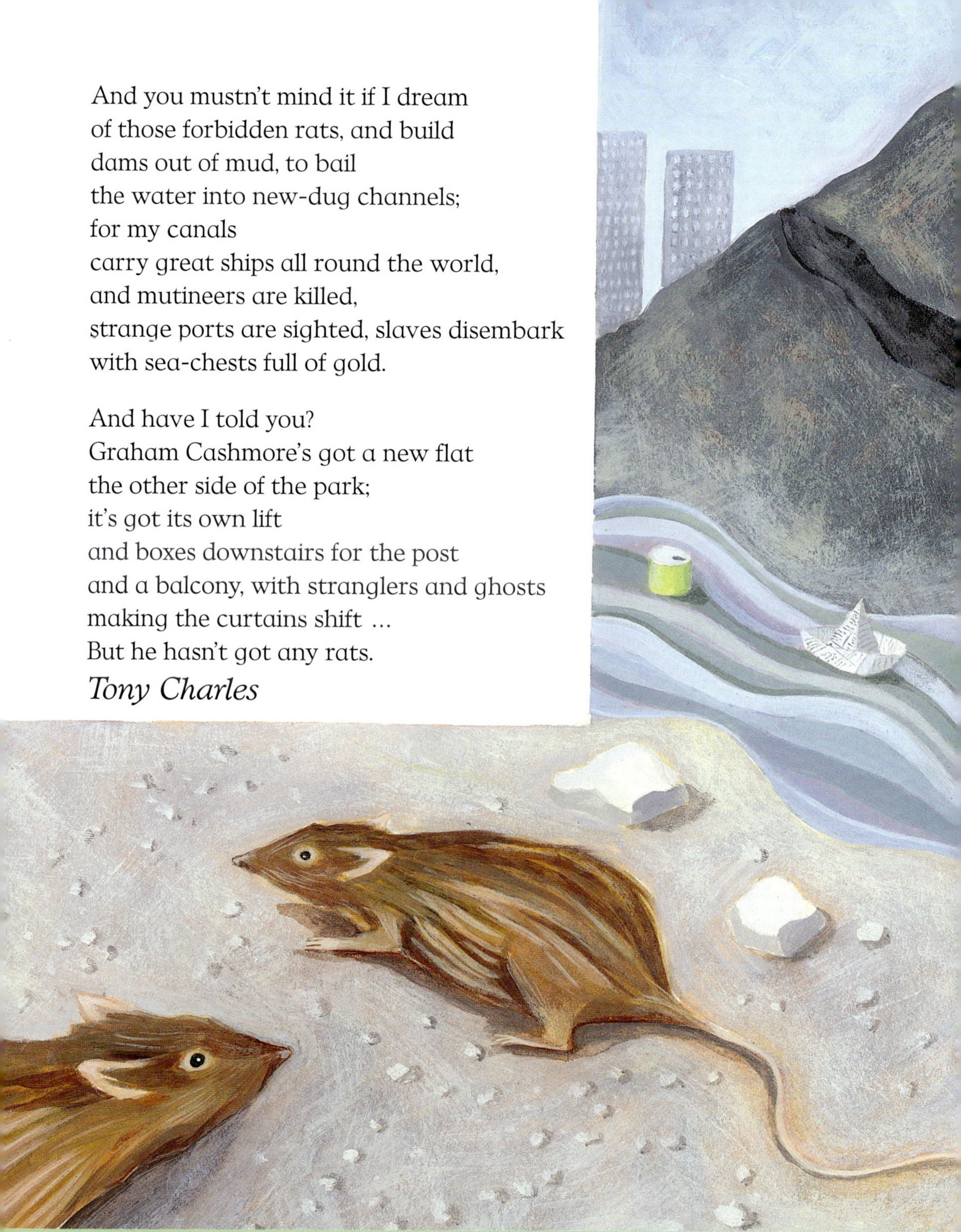

 Did anything change when you read it?

City Jungle

Rain splinters town.

Lizard cars cruise by;
their radiators grin.

Thin headlights stare –
shop doorways keep
their mouths shut.

At the roadside
hunched houses cough.

Newspapers shuffle by,
hands in their pockets.
The gutter gargles.

A motor bike snarls;
Dustbins flinch.

Streetlights bare their
  yellow teeth.
The motorway's
cat-black tongue
lashes across
the glistening back
of the tarmac night.

Pie Corbett

Sing a Song of People

Sing a song of people
Walking fast or slow;
People in the city
Up and down they go.

People on the sidewalk,
People on the bus;
People passing, passing,
In back and front of us.
People on the subway
Underneath the ground;
People riding taxis
Round and round and round.

People with their hats on,
Going in the doors,
People with umbrellas
When it rains and pours.
People in tall buildings
And in stores below;
Riding elevators
Up and down they go.

What pictures do you get of the city in this poem?

People walking singly,
People in a crowd;
People saying nothing,
People talking loud.
People laughing, smiling,
Grumpy people too;
People who just hurry
And never look at you!

Sing a song of people
Who like to come and go;
Sing of city people
You see but never know.
Lois Lenski

Are they different from those in City Jungle? Which poem do you prefer?

Keeping Krindlekrax

Caring for

Feeding

Grooming

Teaching tricks